OF COURSE TENNIS

P. J. Parsons

To Jan.

Best Wishes

Peter P.

May 2015.

ARTHUR H. STOCKWELL LTD
Torrs Park, Ilfracombe, Devon, EX34 8BA
Established 1898
www.ahstockwell.co.uk

British Library Cataloguing-in-Publication Data.
A catalogue record for this book is available
from the British Library.

My thanks to the beaver behind the scenes,
my daughter Dawn, for her support.

ISBN 978-0-7223-4513-9
Printed in Great Britain by
Arthur H. Stockwell Ltd
Torrs Park   Ilfracombe
Devon EX34 8BA

PROLOGUE

Throughout the UK there exist numerous small and medium-sized tennis clubs run almost entirely by volunteers whose generally thankless task is to keep the game of tennis alive in their particular area. They thereby encourage the participation in sport of a variety of individuals with some interest in exercise.

Despite the modern desire for individual mechanical exercise in comfortable indoor surroundings there is still a comprehensive network of these clubs, where sport can be enjoyed and social interaction achieved at a generally reasonable cost.

Such tennis clubs, ranging in size from the one- or two-court small village clubs to the six-to-eight-court giants, provide an opportunity for athletic and semi-athletic individuals of all ages to display their aptitude for some outdoor physical activity.

On any given summer evening and at weekends these energetic individuals may be seen executing a variety of movements and shots loosely related to tennis.

Various loans and occasional grants to the larger clubs, generally with a raft of conditions relating to junior membership, have had to date little effect on the desire to produce players of the highest calibre in substantial

3

numbers. However, there are those who, together with the sighting of the first cuckoo, have reported the appearance of the green shoots of recovery in this respect. The consensus of opinion from the sages of the bar is that this view is a triumph of optimism over experience.

In keeping with the democratic ethos most but not all of these clubs are run by a committee elected by the members, with the various offices being filled by press-ganged volunteers, occasionally supplemented by a co-opted ordinary member to obtain a quorum.

Without these clubs and their committees there is no doubt that, for some, exercise would be restricted to the fingers operating the remote control of the TV, giving rise to a new medical condition to be known as RFS (repetitive finger syndrome) – with consequent effects, particularly for unhappy motorists.

THE COMMITTEE

The difficulties of standing down or resigning once elected to office are a factor in those members who are aware of these hazards not accepting nomination.

To overcome this situation, clubs have introduced specific periods in office in order that there is a fairly regular change in the committee.

Nominations for election to the committee are largely based upon flattery and persistent persuasion. In the first instance it is necessary to overcome the general torpor of members who prefer to plough their own furrow, or perhaps no furrow at all.

Inevitably there will be at least one member who, without wishing to share his vast knowledge with the entire club through the committee, is prepared (generally with hindsight) to advise anyone who is prepared to listen where the committee is at fault. Needless to say, his advice will be proffered well into the evening around the club bar. Strangely, the opportunity to air this advice within earshot of the committee or at the annual general meeting will not be taken.

The public face of the committee – i.e. the AGM – is an opportunity to meet face-to-face with those members who choose or have to be coerced to attend. For some it is also an opportunity to publicise how passionate they are about their club and to establish that nothing revolutionary is being planned.

The possibility of consensus at some AGMs which are not well attended is assisted by an equality of numbers on both sides of the table, despite the inclusion on the committee of the co-opted member.

While for some appointment or election to office is a source of ego satisfaction, particularly when they have the title of 'chairman', for most reluctant nominees committee work means hard and often thankless efforts on behalf of their club, a fact regrettably not fully recognised by some club members.

PRESIDENT

The position of president is normally occupied by a retired or semi-retired, in the tennis sense, former grandee unknown to the majority of club members.

Generally this is a non-active role, restricted to a once-a-year appearance at either a social function of importance or, occasionally, an AGM.

Often the president is awarded this position subject to committee approval in recognition of past services and the ability to remember some of the names of members – especially those who have been members for twenty years or more.

Acceptance of this highly coveted title can sometimes be influenced by the possibility of perks. These may include an appearance adjacent to the Royal Box at Wimbledon or attendance at the bar when the notoriously shy member offers to buy a drink. It has to be said that long odds are laid against such events occurring.

CHAIRMAN

For some of the more traditional and smaller clubs, the filtering through of terminology concerning equality has resulted in the title of 'chairman' remaining although the position is often filled by a lady member of the club.

The common view of members is that this position is best occupied by an individual possessing the qualities of infinite tact and diplomacy combined with the authority of the prime minister and the hide of a rhinoceros.

Whilst the post is occasionally occupied by an enthusiastic egocentric member, for the most part tennis-club chairmen are enthusiastic and influential heads of committee who are prepared to put in a great deal of effort on behalf of their tennis club.

The AGM, for the members who attend, is the only opportunity to observe the chairman since most of the chairman's duties are performed out of members' view at committee meetings, but the influence of a positive and keen chairman is essential to a well-established club.

TREASURER

The treasurer (occasionally known as 'honorary treasurer') should have some connection with figures other than those of some of the lady or sometimes men members. A thick skin is essential in rebutting the association of expensive holidays with a coincident fall in the club's finances.

Unusual incidents involving treasurers do occasionally raise eyebrows. These incidents include spontaneous combustion at a club treasurer's house where, mysteriously, the only item damaged or destroyed by fire was the club's financial accounts book; the remainder of the house was untouched.

In some smaller clubs the lack of volunteers means that some posts are combined. This occurred in a small village club where the zeal of the combined secretary/treasurer was legendary. Regrettably her timing was occasionally inconvenient and thus she acquired the name Contraceptive Constance – she would pursue the payment of match and tournament fees at almost any hour of the day or night, and this had the unwanted side effect that the village birth rate remained below average.

Presentation of the balance sheet at the AGM can, depending on the circumstances, be the highlight or lowlight of the year for the treasurer.

The eye for a chance demonstrated by the treasurer of one club, who persuaded a young lady of agreeable disposition to carry out bar duties, was immediately rewarded with an upsurge in bar takings and a consequent rise in barfly numbers. The technique became known as the honeypot tactic.

SECRETARY

The most underrated member of the main committee, the secretary is generally the most conscientious of club members since his or her task involves almost every aspect of the day-to-day running of the tennis club.

In smaller clubs with a less-structured committee the duties of social secretary and treasurer are combined to form one position.

The catch-22 situation for any efficient and competent secretary is that efficiency can lead to re-election on a fairly regular basis.

At one smaller club the secretary undertook the duties of three-quarters of the committee; consequently, club matters and affairs became a dictatorial operation.

SOCIAL SECRETARY

The elected (press-ganged) member who fills the position of social secretary is responsible for organising various events, such as discos, quizzes, barbecues and the festivities on Club Finals Day. All such events are closely monitored by the honorary treasurer, whose idea of a successful social function is one which involves 400% profit for the club.

The major problem for most social secretaries is to sell ideas for events to the club members. This is especially difficult if the proposed event is outside the range of normal functions. Later, together with other committee members, the social secretary has to persuade the honorary treasurer to spend at least some of the proceeds – this, of course, presumes the function has actually made a profit.

For the most part, holders of this coveted position are imbued with rampant optimism that the mass enthusiasm of the club members will result in success for a particular event.

The high point of the social secretary's calendar is the inevitable Christmas party, since it signals the end of his or her organisational duties for that particular year and the next social events are some months away.

FIXTURES SECRETARY

The introduction of computers has changed the efficiency with which inter-club fixtures are arranged, but the problems are not entirely eliminated since different clubs have fixtures secretaries with different levels of competence. Thus it is still possible to arrive at a particular club on a cold November morning to be told that the day's fixture has been rearranged for next or last week.

Computer-generated fixture lists do not, however, take account of the tendency of various members to develop coughs, colds or headaches at short notice. These ailments normally afflict the individual before away matches – with the severity of symptoms depending on travelling distance – and disappear for home fixtures.

Coping with members' fluctuating health problems is the most difficult problem in fulfilling the office of fixtures secretary. In some of the less well-endowed clubs the difficulties are multiplied by the inclusion of club-tournament dates within the duties of the fixtures secretary.

CAPTAIN

The captaincy of the team or teams to represent the club provides an opportunity to indulge personal preferences; in some cases the captain has automatic selection to play with the partner of his or her choice. Since the majority of matches are played in a doubles format, the possession of a degree in PYP (pick your partner) is very useful in ensuring continuity of selection.

The actual playing time on court for some captains is often surpassed by the time spent in collection of match fees, provision of refreshment, and retention for further use of the used match balls.

Co-ordination and contact between the various teams, particularly those with fixtures on the same weekend, is spasmodic in some clubs, with the lowest-ranked team bearing the brunt of late withdrawals in the teams above.

The captain of mixed-doubles teams faces problems of a slightly different nature, generally related to avoidance of married-couple partnerships and careful selection of socially compatible pairings.

BAR MEMBER

It is generally considered essential to elect a separate club member to ensure that the club has a well-run and well-stocked bar.

Various suggestions will be offered by those members who actually visit the bar – including most members of the committee – and sometimes those who do not. Requests, other than those involving industrial language, generally relate to a favourite beer or wine, or, from the lightweight drinkers, requests for snacks to soak up the alcohol.

There is little doubt that the bar member who is able to satisfy the majority of club members together with the bar staff is a decided asset – not only to the honorary treasurer, but to the club as a whole.

Lack of stock and the introduction of new types of beer or wines are just two of the potential hazards faced by the bar member, who, under pressure from the honorary treasurer, is also charged with increasing income whilst reducing expenditure.

MEMBERSHIP

The membership of most if not all clubs covers a wide range of individuals. Various professions and trades will be represented, including legal beagles with a penchant for lengthy discussions and accountants with little apparent knowledge of the scoring system. Executives and company chairmen can often become less than authoritative when faced with decisions during a game of tennis. Insurance personnel who are unable to read the small print concerning the rules of tennis are a constant source of derision and amusement to some club members. Passion and temperament which are absent from the workplace often become evident within the confines of a tennis court.

One aspect of tennis club membership, which is in decline, is the playing-in of a prospective member with a suitable opponent from the committee. In the event that the standard of the prospective member is slightly higher than the opponent's the advice is for the newcomer to suffer marginal defeat in a closely fought encounter, thus not embarrassing the said committee opponent. On the whole the assimilation of new members is a painless operation largely dependent on the individuals concerned and their ability to socialise.

For junior members, membership normally begins with playing parents or group-coaching sessions with their peers. For the most part it is a separate existence with little contact with the general membership. Tolerance and encouragement, which should be the norm, is, with some diehard senior members, anything but.

Specific playing times are one of the measures that the juniors have to accept until their invitation to 'join the crowd' is made by a senior. This can occasionally lead to exchanges of the sort which occurred at one club. The junior having been approached to confirm his age (i.e. sixteen or over as he was on court after the six-o'clock watershed), responded with the remark, "Well, sir, I am nearer sixteen than you are." A rare example of a humorous remark from a teenager to a senior!

It is quite common for the clubhouse to be filled with the aroma of fish and chips or burgers purchased and eaten on the premises by the juniors after a hard day's graft at school. Regrettably with the discovery of other delights, mainly connected with meeting the opposite sex, their interest in tennis diminishes.

It is not considered strange, in some instances, for juniors to continue their discussions on tennis-court tactics under the table-tennis table or in the kitchen. For these discussions the absence of seniors is of course preferable. The official definition of this is extracurricular activity or specialised homework.

LADIES

Unlike some other sports, there are few, if any, single-sex tennis clubs. The majority of tennis clubs contain a fair representation of mixed membership. One effect of the presence of lady members is to temper the use of industrial language, particularly on court and around the bar, although some lady members have been known to stray into what is known as unladylike behaviour.

Without the presence of these lady members there is no doubt that the majority of the non-committee tasks would not take place. Their generally conscientious adherence to the club afternoon tea rotas is just one example, and there are many others.

The occasional dispute regarding equality law, particularly in club sessions, is normally resolved without recourse to higher authority – generally a committee member with a knowledge of ancient club rules.

The existence and support of a thriving female membership is an essential part of any well-run tennis club.

MEN

The archaic term 'gentlemen members' is no longer in everyday use since, in the first instance, it is difficult to justify use of the word to describe at least some of the male members.

For the younger generation (those under the age of seventy-five), the term is almost an insult to their modern macho image – always assuming they know the true meaning of the word.

In general the men bring many benefits to the tennis club – not only with their representation on the committee, but also with their contribution to the club's finances through their activities at the bar.

VETERANS

The word 'veteran' may be used to describe a junior who is a veteran of numerous matches and tournaments or anyone over the age of thirty-five.

In the younger age group it could be considered complimentary, but the term generally refers to one whose edge of speed has diminished over the years.

The fact remains that pairings of veterans against those in a lower age bracket can sometimes lead to embarrassment for the younger players since the veterans have of necessity substituted guile and position for speed. The basic premise for the veteran player is to place the ball where the opponent is not.

The playing life of a veteran has been greatly prolonged by the advance of medical science. It is now quite common to hear of parts worn with age and usage being replaced. These include new knees and hips. Orthopaedic operations for backs, shoulders, etc., eye operations and new improved pacemakers have continued the trend.

For those members with an hour or so to spend, an enquiry about the health of a veteran can often lead to a detailed description of the condition, including the exhaustive particulars of operations, and the latest information on wonder cures and diets. Since club membership covers a wide range of professions and trades it has been known for the bored and mischievous listener to refer one of these veterans to a new member for advice and possible treatment, only for him to discover the new member is in fact a semi-retired veterinary surgeon. Whilst it is common for such veterans to remember exact details of their own medical treatment, their attention to detail together with memory recall is often absent in the heat of a game of tennis. In doubles it is not unusual for each of the quartet to have a different idea of the score.

The combined effect of details of medical problems and possibly hazy self-complimentary details of past glories has often led to listeners being afflicted by nausea, headaches and temporary partial deafness.

LIFE MEMBERSHIP

In a number of clubs the membership includes a relatively small number who the committee have decided should be offered membership for life following payment of a one-off membership fee. There are a variety of reasons for electing life members, ranging from the honorary treasurer's eye for a quick profit, based upon the member's appearance, to the ego-centred award to an ex-chairman.

It has been known for life members who are considered past their sell-by date to attend AGMs and vote for an increase in annual membership fees, they of course being unaffected.

CLUB SESSIONS

Club nights or club afternoons are generally restricted to one evening during the week and, traditionally, Saturday afternoons. The format allows for the majority of members who are at business during the day to have their exercise in the company of other club members. This results in a complete mixture of ages and sexes, with the opportunity for a member to test his or her ability with other members. The protocol for these sessions varies considerably and is subject to alteration at short notice.

Although in theory these are all-together occasions, there is also an opportunity for some members to circumvent this by various methods of deviousness in order that they may compete with or against their particular choice of partner or opponent. The machinations of these individuals would do credit to the most shifty of politicians, temporary fatigue or injury being just one of the reasons for refusal to participate at a particular moment.

Each club has its own methods of attempting to overcome this issue with optimistic solutions, such as ladders, lists, stewards, and the occasional input and supervision by the club coach. The method employed by one club coach in particular, whilst admittedly unorthodox, created a problem of its own. The procedure adopted was to collect the rackets of those assembled and throw them into the air, forming a jumble of tennis rackets from which he would select four at random. This quartet were then allocated a free court. The resultant confusion over the ownership of the rackets resulted in a lengthy delay. It was later considered that this attempt to avoid favouritism and demonstrate club togetherness was not worth repetition.

The wealthier and more organised of clubs include a system where tennis balls are provided by the club. Some clubs, however, rely upon the members producing their own balls for play during club sessions. This unfortunately allows an opportunity for a minority to avoid further expense in this connection. Reasons given by these frugal members for the non-production of tennis balls might include the appetite of the family dog for tennis balls, balls being left in the 'other' tennis bag and, most originally, balls being mistaken and taken for eggs by a low-flying stork. The response of other members to these comments, whilst generally unprintable, included the remark that perhaps these balls had been dyed the same colour as the court and therefore rendered invisible.

Having somehow, after months or years of pressure, managed to persuade a member to provide tennis balls which were less than five years old and did actually bounce, it was a source of much amusement whenever a ball was missing at the end of play. This resulted in the ball provider searching long into the night and, occasionally, the next day for the absent heirloom. It was later confirmed that the local fire brigade was not enlisted in the search.

For the morally upright and careful, the marking of tennis balls is essential, although this does not always overcome the missing-ball problem.

The various styles of tennis can be a source of entertainment in themselves.

The clothing of players, with styles ranging from younger members (anything goes) to the veterans (keep up with the times), covers the full range of colours and trends. The more traditional clubs who are attempting to retain a whites-only Wimbledon ethic are increasingly rare, and the relaxation in most clubs has resulted in rainbow-coloured tennis equipment, including rackets and shoes.

Amongst lady members, fashion statements are an essential part of participation, ranging in effect from the sublime to occasionally the optimistic.

In the case of veterans, normal tennis clothing is often supplemented by a variety of medical aids, including arm, wrist and knee bandages. Such is the extent of these aids that the identity of the individual is sometimes difficult to establish.

The general rule with tennis clothing, however, is juniors, predominantly non-white; seniors, variety; veterans, following fashion; ladies, anything fashionable; and diehards, white only.

The choice of style of play is equally diverse. The acceptance or otherwise of coaching advice is evident on the tennis court. Service actions in particular range from the marionette (in which the right arm and the left leg appear to be joined by strings) to the semaphore (where both arms and both legs operate to produce what could be described as a serve). Positions for the delivery of a service also vary considerably. They range from far right to far left to in the centre and can be anywhere near the baseline. My experience is that, even in competitive play, foot faults are rarely called, except possibly when the server's foot touches the service line.

For younger players the pleasure in producing one service ace in approximately forty attempts is enough to spur them to continue the same technique.

Optimism springs eternal, however, and one senior member who achieved double figures on a service-speed-monitoring machine was consequently touted as being on the edge of the professional circuit.

Club afternoons and evenings are the backbone of the club and reflect the status and enthusiasm of the members. While the hotshots and some of the would-be hotshots may deem their appearance at these events unnecessary, for most ordinary members this is an opportunity to demonstrate their aptitude and to enjoy the sport.

At any given club session it is possible to observe a full range of shots being attempted and sometimes executed. Backhand slices, approach shots, topspin returns and forehand lobs all make their appearance, either by accident or design. The absence of hotshots is generally accepted, with the occasional comment that even the hotshots of today were the rabbits of yesterday.

Another feature of these club sessions is the provision of afternoon tea undertaken by a club member listed on the tea rota – a duty shared, in theory, by all participants. The standard and variety of the sandwiches and cakes on offer is generally related to the fact that while lady members provide refreshments with variety and substance, the choice provided by male members ranges from the bizarre to the inedible, and invariably includes a request for the bar to be opened up.

TOURNAMENTS/MATCHES

Matches comprising men's, mixed and ladies' doubles are generally scheduled to take place at weekends. Summer and winter fixtures lists occasionally overlap owing to the secretary's inability to differentiate between summer and winter in terms of weather.

The perennial difficulty of a team captain for these matches is in finding a sufficient number of members who are available and willing to participate – not only in the comfortable, accessible and convenient home fixtures, but also in the rather more inconvenient away fixtures – especially in winter. Having selected and obtained the services of four willing participants the experienced captain then confirms the venue, the opponent team and, in the case of home fixtures, that food will be provided. Limited imagination in relation to food invariably means that cheese-and-pickle sandwiches will be a staple in the case of mens' fixtures; more imaginative fillings tend to accompany ladies' and mixed matches. On occasions when ladies organise the catering, a lack of price stamps and Cellophane shop wrapping is noticeable as is an improvement in taste and presentation. Newly selected, inexperienced players may sometimes depart from the norm and provide such exotic choices as peanut-butter-

and-apple or prawn-and-asparagus, much to the delight of the opposition.

The cancellation or postponement of a match does not always prevent some sort of match taking place. On at least one occasion, in a particular kind of mixed-doubles fixture, the two couples merely rearranged their activities in another location.

The build-up to the climax of the club season features the tournaments, which cover almost all types of membership. The appearance of the list of events on the club noticeboard often provokes a frenzy of apathy from all but the most dedicated of pot hunters. Many of these lists with their optimistic publication of specific dates can remain devoid of names for weeks while members consider the options.

Flattery and persuasion is essential in order to prevent the first round and the final of an event being played on the same date. This is particularly true of an event known as the Families Cup. Participation in this event is likened to a part of the Immigration Bill which refers to the fact that if you have been here long enough you must be related to somebody. Having obtained some entries and discussed the seedings and pairings with the more interested of the club members, it is now necessary for the fixtures secretary to ensure that matches are played in roughly the same year as the publication of the draw.

It comes as no surprise that members who are available to play social tennis at the drop of a hat and in all weathers suddenly become reluctant to perform on anything other than a perfect summer day at a time when the inconvenience factor is almost absent.

The publication of the draw is also an opportunity for tournament experts to bring into play a well-worn strategy primarily aimed at reaching the final and gaining a trophy without the tedious process of actually playing a match, or by playing the smallest possible number of matches. This strategy involves stretching the effective or ineffective tournament organiser's patience to the absolute limit by shuffling dates, thus achieving the ultimate objective of a walkover and avoiding the nightmare of defeat. This course of brinkmanship is normally only for the experienced campaigner since there is always the dreaded possibility of the tournament organiser losing patience and actually defaulting the participant. The problem for the tournament organiser is even worse (and the strategy is employed with greater effect) when the matches in question involve four participants.

Finals Day represents in a lot of clubs the end of the tournament organiser's struggle to provide an end-of-season finale of some substance, having overcome the traditional problems of summer in the UK, having gained, as far as possible, the support of the participants.

Attendance at Finals Day is dependent upon weather conditions and the desire of members to be entertained by high-class tennis. Finals Day at one small village club comprised two adults and a small child, and their plucky attempt at a Mexican wave was abandoned after one attempt.

It is not uncommon at the close of the Finals Day jollifications to note that the tournament organiser is too exhausted to participate in the presentation of the trophies. The formerly enthusiastic and optimistic individual will now have become someone of a more sober, realistic nature with a consequent change in appearance. Merely to mention the next year's tournament could cause an extreme reaction and a resort to a bottle of aspirin.

Final mutterings of some of the members in attendance – particularly the runners-up in the various tournaments –

usually include references, occasionally complimentary, concerning the performance of the brave souls enlisted as umpires.

No less keenly fought than the seniors' finals are the juniors' finals. For the subsequent winners Finals Day ends with Bragging Night.

For those with incredible optimism and stamina, fancy-dress tournaments would enable members to exercise their flair for design and fashion; for others, no change of attire would be necessary. Due to the random nature of tennis clothing – among the juniors in particular – fancy-dress tournaments are rarely held.

SOCIAL EVENTS

The various events organised by the social secretary and backed by a willing and enthusiastic membership are, together with membership fees and bar takings, a prime source of finance for most clubs.

The range and diversity of these functions is almost entirely dependent on the flair and ingenuity of the social secretary and his or her ability to attract vast numbers of members to the club room for the first-class entertainment provided.

For those attending discos it is an opportunity to study the various movements employed on the dance floor, some of which are almost identical to the gyrations on the tennis court. The main difference is the lack of a tennis racket; in some cases clothing changes only slightly. The lack of co-ordination shown on the tennis court can make an almost magical return when accompanied by music at a disco.

Occasionally ordinary members may organise separate events, but since these are generally not published and do not generate funds for the club the social secretary does not usually become involved.

On rare occasions the efforts of the social secretary may founder on the rock of torpor among the members.

Then the sound of the disc jockey's patter, with its "Nice to see you all here!" echoing around an almost empty club room, may cause the social secretary to beat a hasty retreat to the bar to join the ever present barflies.

THE CLUBHOUSE AND BAR

The variety and size of tennis clubs is reflected to some extent in the clubhouse itself. These range from the eight-court club's modern, plush, purpose-built clubhouse to the somewhat less salubrious large garden shed of the smaller village club.

Most clubhouses are littered with various notices, advertising tournaments and forthcoming events, supplemented by honours boards of past champions. In most clubs the club bar is second only to the courts as a prime asset. The sophistication and age of the clubhouse furniture and furnishings can reflect the efforts of various committees over their years of tenure. Provision of clubhouse furniture can vary dramatically from the modern sleek and colourful furniture of the wealthy club to the period furniture of the late-jumble-sale/early-bonfire type of the impoverished smaller club. The observation that this type of furniture enables some members to blend with their surroundings is in some cases a valid point.

The protective instinct of a committee member in a club where new modern furniture had been installed led to an exchange with a mature ladies' doubles team following their exertions on court and their consequent desire to rest on a new banquette. Having observed that the proximity of damp tennis clothing to the new furniture could have some adverse effect, the committee member was advised that no perspiration was involved in this particular quartet's activities.

The objective for successive committees is to provide surroundings which reflect the character and individuality of their club.

The bar itself is for some the focal point of the club and for others a virtual minefield to be approached warily. It relies primarily on its practicality rather than its appearance, and in general its decor does not contribute significantly to the club's prestige. Service and accessibility is the prime requirement for the members, coupled with necessary security to prevent self-service.

The bar is manned by club members and supervised by the bar manager, and their qualifications must include international-class diplomacy, infinite patience and resistance to flattery concerning last orders. Ideal bar staff must have the ability to feign interest in a story or joke which they have heard repeatedly over the last three years, the discretion of a father confessor and an apparent Swiss-style neutrality. Venturing an opinion can sometimes be unwise. In general adopting the motto *tutuum silentii praemium* (silence is golden) is a safe bet – especially beneficial when confronted by a late-night group of barrack-room lawyers.

The sheer persistence of some barflies in repeating stories which are neither humorous nor original despite constant barracking from fellow drinkers tests the patience and diplomacy of bar staff well beyond the call of duty.

MEMBERS OF THE BAR

The club bar generally attracts a variety of members wishing perhaps to buy a drink or, occasionally, to give attendant members the benefit of their opinions or expertise. These gatherings may also include the reluctant visitor.

Among the regulars, further classifications include the Storyteller, the Joke Teller, the Wise Old Owl, the Fount of All Knowledge and, in recent times, the Gadget Master. In even the smallest of groups you will generally find a barrack-room lawyer with the Fount of All Knowledge in general opposition on a variety of current issues.

AROUND THE BAR

Among the predominantly male clientele, topics range from the price of beer through character assassination of absent members to whichever topic the most prominent (loudest) barrack-room lawyer decides is topical. The lucidity and logic of the various topics discussed around the bar is entirely dependent on the time of the discussion (the amount of drinking time which has passed), and debate is generally terminated by the slamming of the bar shutters and the rattling of keys by the bar member. Multiple conversations and discussions can often lead to a sober listener becoming completely bewildered. Remarks regarding the latest match results often collide in mid sentence with remarks about the merits of a particular bottled beer.

The ultimate show-stopper on these occasions is the intervention of a long-standing member with a desire to repeat a 'new' story or joke – a story or joke which can be repeated word for word by almost every member of the club.

Salacious tales of unofficial mixed doubles being continued despite the failure of the floodlights, stories of rowdy 'Bat 'n' Beer' tournaments continuing long after dark . . . Each club has its legends, and nostalgia is a common factor.

For the experienced and vociferous barfly, securing the most advantageous position to project their views and air their undoubted knowledge on all subjects is essential. The infiltration of a new member into these post-play forums is generally allowed on the understanding that this member should observe the three-to-six-months no-speaking rule. Acceptance of this member is often related to his willingness to buy a round of drinks.

Lifelong friendships may be formed in half an hour, although these may not be evident the following week.

The repeated manoeuvres of regular barflies include attempts to force the shy on-the-fringe drinker to buy a round. Often a member about to leave will change his mind upon hearing the forced whispered comment, "It is my round." He will then make a hasty return in order to celebrate this event.

The topics for discussion by assembled barflies are unpredictable. In one rural club discussion concerned the provision of memorial garden benches for expired long-servicing members. One long-standing life member was surprised to find almost unanimous support for his memorial-bench idea, only to discover that it was the opportunity to sit on a bench dedicated to him which evoked this support.

OVERSEAS CLUBS

Overseas clubs are generally set up by former expert tennis players and are run and organised as far as possible on the same lines as clubs in the UK. Various differences occur, however, mainly owing to different weather patterns. This is particularly noticeable in warmer climates. Members who have in the past volunteered to clear snow from the lines are now called upon to cope with the monsoon season.

Dress code can range from the diehards' only whites to newcomers' (particularly lady members') latest fashions and the eccentrics' (particularly old colonial hands') khaki shorts and long socks. Dress code is sometimes supplemented by visiting juniors with a disregard for anything normal.

In overseas clubs new opportunities exist for gamesmanship exponents. They are now able to specify locusts, snakes and heat haze in order to gain some respite or advantage.

In some of the older overseas clubs visitors' books are still in use, giving visitors an opportunity for general comment. In one such club the remark made in 1939 that the club flagpole required attention and the pennant needed to be replaced was repeated by the same visitor in 1946 with the comment that to date the committee had still taken no action on the matter. It is believed that the visitor had recently returned to the tennis world following an enforced and unavoidable incarceration lasting some years. Since the club in question had on one occasion at an extraordinary general meeting (EGM) spent some three hours debating the difference between a serviette and a napkin, the issue of the flagpole was not considered to be worthy of comment.

An example of the traditional nature of one overseas club was shown when a tennis member appeared in cream-coloured clothing despite the whites-only regulation established in club rules. For some months the offending member was studiously ignored by some other members whenever he entered the club room.

GAMESMANSHIP

A facet of the game which has existed since tennis was first played, gamesmanship is practised with varying degrees of success at every level of the game.

At the highest professional level it can include a judicious comfort break (accompanied), a timely and apparently spontaneous coughing or sneezing fit when the opponent is about to serve, or a wave to a passing friend before a crucial point.

Significantly some players who have partial deafness when the phrase "It's your round" is mentioned are often disturbed by birdsong or a dog barking some distance from the court.

At rural clubs gamesmanship opportunities may be provided by smoke from an adjacent garden bonfire, gusts of wind among the leaves of trees and squirrels on the fence. Any and all of these can elicit the staple plea of a player in some difficulty: "Let, please!" – sometimes a request and occasionally a demand.

Rearrangements at short notice of starting times for matches and the use of tennis balls discarded by a family dog can provide extra scope for gamesmanship, with an air of surprise at any subsequent comment or objection.

Synthetic sportsmanship is evident when a player

accedes to a disputed call when leading at 40–love but will never do the same when the positions are reversed.

By virtue of their comparative longevity in the game, veterans have adapted and enhanced the potential for gamesmanship by various specific methods. Faced by an opponent wearing the contents of a medium-sized shop specialising in medical and surgical aids, the younger opponent with a charitable nature may well drop his guard, only to find that his hampered, mechanically aided opponent has the speed of a gazelle and the constitution of a lion. Sometimes even the eyesight appears to be virtually perfect.

There is little doubt that if the Garden of Eden had included a tennis court, Adam would have resorted to the shoelace trick, used to recover breath during exertion or stress – possibly the oldest and most well-used gamesmanship manoeuvre in the sport.

GLOSSARY OF TERMS

SWEET SPOT   Any part of the racket frame or handle

LOVE   Generally self-directed; alternatively, off-court affairs

LINES   Court markings, variable in width and occasionally invisible

DEUCE   Inability to remember the actual score

VOLLEY   Abuse

HALF-VOLLEY   Half-hearted abuse

LET   Sportingly offer to replay the point after being beaten by the shot or serve

COMPETITIVE PLAYER   One who cheats whenever possible

SOCIAL PLAYER   One who hardly ever wins

THROW UP	Result of previous evening's social activity at the bar
SPIN	Opportunity in social doubles to discard a dodgy partner
PYP	The sheer coincidence of being paired with the best available partner
MIXED DOUBLES	Men's singles with interference
MEN'S SINGLES	Warfare between the myopic and those with long-range vision
BEGINNERS	Rabbits
BALLS	See *Volley*
RACKET HANDLE	Used to perform upper and lower endoscopy on opponent
GRIP	Normally connected with throat
THROAT	See *Grip*
CALLS	Contact with friends during play, generally via mobile phone
UMPIRE	Three categories: 1, Richard the Lionheart for accepting the position; 2, Mother Teresa; and 3, Attila the Hun
LINESMAN	Recreation for the insomniac

SHORTS	Suitable for wear by one player in 500 who wish to look elegant
SKIRTS	Opportunity to display legs that could support a snooker table
SPIN	Recounting of post-match exploits, generally with some poetic licence
TOPSPIN	Lengthy version of the above (see *Spin*), narrated to incredulous listeners and subject to repetition

ISOLATION

The emergence on a fairly regular basis of the letters GB at the top end of the world rankings has had the effect of changing the views of the sages of the bar from "cloud cuckoo land" to "I told you so", thus preserving their status as members of the Hindsight Society. The well-deserved British player at the top of the sport is a certain Mr Murray and the subject on everyone's lips is *Of Course Tennis*.